Balance

New and Selected Poems

by

DANIEL THOMAS MORAN

Cyberwit.net
HIG 45 Kaushambi Kunj, Kalindipuram
Allahabad - 211011 (U.P.) India
http://www.cyberwit.net
Tel: +(91) 9415091004 +(91) (532) 2552257
E-mail: info@cyberwit.net

Printed at Repro India Limited.

This book is dedicated to my friends,

Charles Noon lll and Elizabeth Knies Storm,

and as always, to Karen

Acknowledgments

Some of the poems is this collection have been previously published in the following journals: *Poetry Salzburg Review* (Austria), *The Humanist, Columbia Journal, Contemporary Literature Review India, Exit 13, Hektoen International, Here in the Afterlife* (2017 Integral Contemporary Literature Press (Bucharest, Romania), *FEKT* (Kosovo), *Journal of The Visuality and Mathematics Conference (Belgrade, Serbia), The Henniker Review, Ekphrasis Project-Joost de Jonge* (Amsterdam, The Netherlands), *Journal of Dental Humanities, Levure Litteraire* (Par is, France), *Like Light: 25 Years of Poetry and Prose* (Br ight Hill Press), *Lit.Cat, Literary Matters – The Journal of The Association of Literary Scholars, Critics and Writers, Even the Daybreak: 35 Years of Salmon Poetry 35th Anniversary Anthology* (Salmon Poetry, Ireland), *The Same, New Contrast: South African Literary Journal, Universal Oneness: An Anthology of Magnum Opus Poems From Around The World* (India) and *VIA: Voices in Italian Americana* (Bordighera Press) and Salmon Poetry (Ireland).

Contents

The Song of Adam

Beneath
these ribs
I bear
a mark
Where I tore
my belly
Upon
the dark.

Between
flesh & forever
I could
not doubt
The dark
came in,
But some light
got out.

To My Young Son

There was that day in October
In a room familiar to no one,
Where your entirety rested
On less than a forearm measure.
My palm a cradle, my fingers
Expressed like new petals
Around your bud of face.
Now you like to adorn yourself
In my shirts and shoes, that
Old leather jacket you found
in the deep of my closet.
You want to stand back to back.
I feel you slide against me
As you lift your heels and
Reach to meet my shoulders.
You cast your palm on mine
And say many hopeful things.
But I tell you to sleep well,
To reach up without fearing.
The day will be upon us soon
When I will need to raise up
my face to see into your eyes.
When I will need to be
Reassured by your shoulders.
Someday I will need to
Call out to you to come close
And make of your hands
A cradle for my head.

Traveling

Sometimes
I take the
long way
home.
To see
what
I have not
been missing.
To be
nearer
those things
I can
do without.
I fulfill
that need
for distance
and
misspent time.
Semi-circles
in exchange for
straight lines.

At Hard Labor

I suppose I am grateful
that writing a poem
is not like mining sulfur
from the banks of a volcano
or welding a crossbeam
miles above the street.
Nor is it like
erecting a dream house.
Most days, it is more
like splicing a phone line,
or hanging a door
on a linen closet.

After all, we live
in a world of toiling,
sweeping the dust
from the steps,
only to find them
wanting once more.
Wiping the gray mud
from our boots, then
walking out into the
field again at morning.

I have never
invited these poems, yet
they keep on arriving
one by one, shaking
the rain

from their shoulders
as they emerge from
the dark beyond my door.
I suppose I am grateful
that they did not
rob my house
or steal my children
from their
very beds.

Writing a poem
is not like
rising at first light
to cook for an army,
but more like
waking at ten on Sunday
to prepare an omelet
for someone you really love,
or teaching a small child
to lace up a shoe.

It is the dancers I pity,
who must aspire
to leap and spin, and
the painters who must
live with the burn of
turpentine in their veins.
What of the man
near the park, who stands
on the best days and the worst
turning chestnuts over tiny coals.
Or the waitress
who must always

be concerned with
what I want to drink.

Writing a poem is not
like any of that, I think.
But enough, the rain
is ferocious tonight,
So much that I fear
the hills will be washed away,
And if I am not mistaken,
there may be someone
at my door.

Creed

The way
puddles dry
after
a night of rain.

The way
I reach up
and balance
the moon
on the tip
of my finger.

The way
a clock
proceeds
in pointless
circles.

The way
your ribs,
without thought,
mimic the tides
while you sleep.

Perhaps,
this is all

I know about
eternity.

Lying with Marianne on St. Mark's Place

In the bookshop on St. Mark's Place
I'm lying with Marianne Moore
Spine to spine, beneath
hard covers, shelved neatly
for posterity by the
motherly fingers of
soft friends.

She loves her men
silent and I love
my ladies profound.
There we lie, poised
in our communal in-
spirations, naked
musings and alliteration.

Often in the padlocked
midnight, I wait for
her to turn and embrace
me but still,
she acts as though she
never even knew me.

Orphans

In this world
orphans beget orphans,
misery throbs
like a distant drum.
If only agony
were bread and
despair
a cool stream.
If only futility
were wisdom and
anguish
a field of sunflowers
stretching to the
copper plum horizon.

Translating Now

for Samuel Menashe

Maintenant,
from *la main,*
the hand,
Wed to
the verb *tenir,*
to hold,
Becomes
maintenant,
That which
one holds
in one's hand.
Not *le passé,*
the past,
That which is
beyond our holding.
Nor *l'avenir,*
the future,
That which
is beyond
our grasping.
But *maintenant,*
the present,
That which
we hold
in our hand,
All we can
ever hold
in our hand.

The Swimming Lesson

Down at the tired shores
of Florence Ave. Beach,
an optimist in green trunks
was instructing us on
how to become swimmers.
We, a dozen or so
scrawny specimens on
an early summer day,
one o'clock sharp.
Up to our tiny thighs
in that oily chill.
We knew there
were secrets, that things
lived beneath it all.
We knew, as we stood,
within minutes
the sandy bottom
would swallow our feet.
Our young mothers
looked on from old blankets,,
proud for unknown reasons.
Then the instructor said,
with great authority,
First thing we'll learn
is the dead man's float.

Some cried, but most tried
facing down
into the briny darkness.

We let the bubbles rise
back across our cheeks.
And we made believe
we had failed
to learn to swim.

The River Might Be a Woman

Here, in the first days
along our share of
the Warner River,
I have begun to believe,
that the river is, perhaps,
a beautiful woman.

Nevertheless, it seems
to be a metaphor
going nowhere. But,

The sight of her,
lying along this gentle slope.
The feeling of her,
reclined in the dark beside me.

It has captivated me
in ways which are
not so obvious, and which
do not lend themselves
to my feeble pryings.

I am content with that.
And I want to be
free to marvel.

But I confess,
I also want to touch it.
As a child wants

to touch a candle flame,
or a draping of
magenta velvet.

And then, as a man,
I want to be inside.

Perhaps It Was Not Mars

Lord of all conflict,
outstanding upon
the new darkness
that July night,
subtle but certain
in that field of star.
Our eyes led
by a way of light
to the profile
of a waxing moon.
Perhaps Saturn,
who plants faith,
or Jupiter, whose
dominance moves
the thunder and skies.
It did not matter.
It was all
there before us.
Nameless and ancient.
Those million
pinholes in
the drape of night.

That moon left
scents for me
in the shadows
on your tender neck.
Until morning,
it was Mercury

god of eloquence,
and Venus ascending,
again and again.

On Compassion

At Darfur
the children, weak
from emptiness,
accord the flies
the tears
from their eyes.

Neither
dares ask mercy
of the dust,
or the
Kings of The World.

God

He is the beginning
and the end.
The bearer of all forevers.
His finger tips
swirl galaxies.
His eye sees
the very codes of life.

With his mercy
He brought forth
purgatory, and
men with two cheeks.
In His wisdom,
He wished a deluge
upon the Earth,
and fashioned Darwin
from the muck.

He is more
than we dare know,
and yet less
than we can imagine.

He made tinmen and popes,
black holes and the aurora borealis.
He is love and
love is blind.
He loves a good fight.
He enjoys His fame.

He had me fail geometry and
made trees which became
the masts of ships, and
the bunks in the death camps.
He conceived of
hummingbirds and nuclear physics.

He is indeed most righteous.
In His firmanent
evil never triumphs.

He makes
plaster madonnas weep and
causes deserts and cancer and
snowflakes and stillbirths and
fireflies and widows and
shadows and the apocalypse.

He knows
everyone by name.
He listens to prayers.
He is the landlord
the taxman and the concierge.
He is surely one
of us.

Christmas Eve at The Waldorf=Astoria

New York City 2006

Jesus brought our bags
up to Room 805
at a little after Three.
He stayed
only long enough
to show us
the mini-bar, and
how to manage
the thermostat.
He let us know
that room service
would bring whatever
we desired.
Around the clock.

He was shorter
than I might have
imagined, from those
paintings of Caravaggio,
and all of the
crucifixes of my childhood.

Hair sable, and newly cut,
He wore a gray uniform,
like the others in His place,
alive to serve mankind.

The outer edge
of His heels were
burnished by the miles
of pavement and carpet.

I wanted to ask Him
about The War,
and the crying babies
in East Harlem.
The dripping glaciers,
and where to find
a thing like Justice
in a world turning itself
inside out.

I wanted to know
if He could ever recall
sixty-three degrees
in New York City, at
the tail end of December.

But, I did not wish
to add to
His burden.
The Lobby
was teeming with
Italians and Minnesotans
and French and
Asians of many kinds.
All staring up
each time the chimes
rolled out from that
fabled golden clock.

There was only time,
to press a folded five
into His palm,
to thank him
for bearing the weight
for us who are travelers.
And He smiled
in a way which
reassured me that
Somehow,
Everything
would be alright.

A History Lesson

We write
our histories
in pencil,
our dreams
in ink.
But time
withers
frail pulp,
much faster
than lead,
much faster
than bled color.
So we must
recall, recite
the drama
of our days,
repeat what
is true
and believed,
over and over
as prayer.

A Poem of Necessity

Today I am grieving, but
not for any certain reason.
It is Saturday at a country house.
No one should be grieving here.

But it happens that way, at times.
It is a thing we do to ourselves.

After all, people sing in prisons.
They laugh in rooms with the dying.
Surely things end, but they
begin as well, don't they?

Perhaps I am not grieving
for today, but for yesterday.
I recall clearly when it was
right there before me, now
I am unsure where I put it.

It is not unlike the wind, which
comes and goes, or the leaves
it takes from these trees, which
accumulate in layers of loss.
It's not for what I can recall,
but only for what I cannot.

It is there in my mirror, in the
face I have come to owning.

The face which has become
a gray shroud for my youth.

So much for us to know,
all the more to be imagined.
Surely we should not
spare time to grieve.
Our time passes, and we
must pass with it.

What strange things, these musing
which can cause the eyes to fill.
Facing how of it much is bygone.

Last night, in this house, our cats
walked the floor above our bed,
through the length of the dark,
while no one was watching,

They traveled the night.

At the Louvre

I've been to see *The Mona Lisa*.
Traversed the angry *Atlantique*.
Dealt with Frenchmen;
their lunging taxis,
their coffee dense and bitter,
their sweet condescension.
I've stood for an hour
in a wind-driven rain.
Descended into the
great pyramid of I.M. Pei.
Paid the fare in francs
to wander that fortress
Past the winged *Victory,*
the armless *Venus,*
Vermeer's *Astronomer.*
Five hundred depictions
of the dying Jesus and
the elegant portraits of
many Frenchmen who
would sadly lose their heads.
I followed the signposts,
heard my heels
down the lengths of
those long hallowed halls.
Then, at once she was there.
Her face looking back at me
over a field of cameras
held high above the crowd.
the subtle *terra incognita* of her

spattered with awe
and battery light.
And I took my turn,
slithered and gaped and
uttered *excuse moi* and
then turned my back again,
and wandered off to
look for *Olympia.*

From the Porch in Summer

That peace we seek, is
that peace we find.
The peace we make.

In the exhalations of sky
upon leaf and limb.
In the ripest berry on the tree,
and the most bitter.

In the journeys which lead nowhere,
and the ones which find us home.
In the reassurance of muted sun
through a thin gauze of cloud.

In the perfect and
uncountable nuances of green.
In the silence beyond speaking and
our surrender to mystery.

In knowing what we must,
what we can, and what

We can not.

This Journey

It is,
of course, one of
the well-worked
metaphors
employed by poets,
The long and pained journey.
The whorl of road ahead.
The grand and stony
insurmountable summit.
The horizon which seems
always to occupy
the most distant point
of our seeing.
Sometimes a stretch
of desert for effect.
The path is always
rocky, muddy after
an endless rain,
Or baked by a sun
without remorse.
There is the fog,
thick as a cataract,
A wind like a
palm, pushing us back.
And we poets
are almost always
going it alone.
The sweet, unbearable
solitude, our crucifix,

our nourishment.
But today,
I will not make
another entry into
the log of my
own many miles,
but say, rather
that I have arrived at
that very place I
once saw in a dream.
It is as I had imagined.
And there was
someone waiting.

Homefires

I'm looking forward
to a place to call home,
with a rack by the door,
to catch my sorry old hat
again, and again.
A familiar aroma
to fill my nostrils.
I'd like a big old chair
to fit my tired self
like a favorite shoe,
near a fire where I can sit,
contemplate my fortunes
and woes,
hold my babes in lap,
and tell them
all the tales I've collected
in the days gone before.
And watch snowflakes
land melting like dreams,
on the big shade tree I
had planted with just
a spade and a palm.

Being

Naked, I
gather a morning
which awakens
these leaves.

Pulse in
my bone
the only
rhythm
I own.

Breaths I
am forming
become one with
the breeze.

At Midnight

A sickle moon
dangles from
a high branch.
Splendor pours
through glass.
The subtle
forms of you
drape across
the frame
of this bedding.
Supple and taut
like a new canvas.
A palette of only
the light and dark.
Then my fingers
create shadows
which weave and spin.
My desire, a dancer.
My love, a ballet.

The Anonymous

for Allen Planz

It is
Saturday night
on Earth, and
within
the subtle
definition of
one thousand
tiny rooms,
filled with
twenty thousand
half empty chairs,
two thousand poets
will offer up
fifty thousand
images
like gemstones
cast by
an imagined sea
upon the sand
of an empty beach.
Not far away,
another
will withdraw
pen from pocket
and endeavor to
summon the divine.

The Man Making Fortune Cookies

In this dim-lit factory

along the broad Chang

where the sweet-air

is hung heavy with the

purple plums of wisdom,

a graying man stands

in The Peoples' Blues

and hand-made sandals,

typing out in red letters,

the futures of us all.

And with ancient ingenuity

weaves them through a

slight curl of confection,

which must also

give up its life

in the end.

In his head

the words of Chuang-tzu

folding over and over

and today like every day

he knows not whether

he is a man

dreaming he is a butterfly

or a butterfly

dreaming he is a man.

Emigrants

for Peter Quinn

One hundred thirty now,
the lingering years gone
since my Moran fled
the pathetic coast
of Mayo, longing toward
some imagined redress.
Today, faces so like
my own, familiar as
whistle and harp notes,
ask, "Have you been?"
and "When will you get
home again?"

Sadly, I cannot say except,
I know I will be there soon.
And when I am, at last, I will
bend to kiss that ground
softly like the forehead
of an aging mother,
Shake hands with a thousand
cousins, listen for the poems
trapped in hill and bog.
I might cast a slackline
for a silver rainbow, smell
the grass at the chapel wall.

Standing before the cliffs,
I'll raise a warm pint of ebony
and foam, and face myself into
the bite of the briny breeze.
To the memory of all my dead,
I'll call out to the back of the sky,
Allowing my blue eyes to moisten
with the pains of the leaving.
I'll recite in tender meter every regret,
and wonder from the bare heights
of the lonesome Connacht shores,
at how it was the wind had
carried us so very far away.

The Giant that Fell on the Man

26 Dec 2019-Hiker Killed by Falling Giant Redwood in Muir Woods

Two hundred feet
is a very long time.
Four feet across, by
an application of ∂,
must be a full dozen
feet round, more rings
than an Indian wedding.

Subhradeep only desired
a long walk along that path,
that courses an untroubled way
thru Muir's red-hearted cathedral.

The tree, having survived
the saws of ten thousand
lumberman, the campfires of
great armies of Boy Scouts, and
the cacophonous horrors that
attended the second millennium,

Wished only to remain plumb,
long enough to reach a few
more branches, up and up thru
the ancient shadows, to prospect
for the Gold of California suns.

In the end, it was only the
weight of raindrops, and the
insufferable consequence of time,
Meeting a man who had a tender
curiosity about a place of giants,
who took five steps too many, or
maybe five steps too few.

Reflection in a Dark Room

for Bryan Lewis

The night that
carried the Beaver Moon,
has raised a new
skin of ice on Ox Pond.
What was yet green
has collapsed, folded
in on itself. Yesterday
was the sharp sun,
a blue clarity to heaven.

Today it is the
many pages of gray,
our Novembers
too many to count.
The day slithers below
the steep of the river hill,
at barely three-fifteen.

Arriving to fill
the empty spaces
the green left behind,
is the junk in our head.
The rubble of a broken
vow, the things that
were just never right,
 a slow unfolding of

memory that can only
strain against itself.

While we hold
tight to one another,
to all we are become,
It lies beside us
in this winter bed, It
lies beside us in
this winter bed, It lies
beside us in this winter
bed.

The Man Who Died Just Before the Pandemic

- March 2020

The man who died
just before the pandemic
was unaware.
No one saw a purpose
in explaining to him
that something far too
small to be dreamed,
had made its way from
a caged animal,
deep into the breaths
of a man who lived in
a place on the other side
of the world, or that
it was coming to find *him*.

The man who died was
too sick himself,
suffering from a body
which had lived
quite long enough.
He did not know that
the world had been
inverted, that everyone
had now come to share
this one thing.

He would not be

among the old and infirm,
who were lying in wait.
He would not be afraid.

The man who died
just before the pandemic
had already folded all of
his life's fears into the
soft hands who held him.
He did not need to
see the evening news, or
the morning news, and
all the many, too many
winded words of distress.

The man who died
just before the pandemic
did not know that
no one would be there
to see him satin-laid
in his dark blue suit.
He did not know that
no one would be there
to gently lower him, or
to toss flowery fronds
into the hole in the Earth
where he would ever sleep.

Perhaps one day,
in a time far off,
when the world
will have reassumed
its bouyant blue balance,

People will recall
the man who died
just before the pandemic,
And that he did so
just in time.

Paris

At six a.m.
Eiffel's Tower is dark,
The garlic of
last night's escargot
still lies on my tongue.

It should
never rain in Paris,
yet it is raining,
The morning's
image drips in
the dim lights.

From this
high window on
the seventeenth floor,
all is anticipation.
The dark boulevards
of this City of Light,
whose names I will
never come to know,

Reach out for the
promises of a rising day.

Ode to Introversion

Philosophers of antiquity
have propounded down through the ages.
As have wisemen, prophets and oracles,
Bodhisattvas, sybils and sages.

Our inscrutable humanity,
has perplexed them and astounded.
Head Shrinkers, soothsayers and gurus,
all confessed they were confounded.

There is one true truth to be embraced,
If we can clear life's junk and see things.
Human beings are best enjoined,
to avoid other human beings.

Forbearance

in isolation, 24 March 2020

Sometimes,
existence alone
is a terrible enough
yoke to shoulder.

I come from
people whose
hearts were large,
people who
understood,
that their breaths
were daily growing
ever more shallow,
and never certain.

My people
carried hammers
and fishing nets,
swords and sickles.
They grasped halyards
and docker's hooks,
wrenches and brooms,
axes and wheels.
They understood,
the many of them,
nothing was but
a shard less than

whatever they had.
They buried babies
and spent many nights
bending at bedsides,
awake and praying
for the fever to break.

My people
stole away no time
for mourning.
The sounds of
a long lament was
in the very walls
that sheltered them.

So now they
have become me,
A man with
no complaint,
A man who has
lived dreams
they had not enough
moments to dream,
A man who spends
his long days
among gifts.

One day,
should it all survive,
I will be looked
back upon, in
some family tree,
and they will say,

Him, yes him.
The one with
the pen and paper.
He was the weak one.

Life Support

I have been to Venice
before the drowning,
before the ancient Aegean
laid her down.
I saw the Galapagos tortoise
alive in its century of shell,
The iguanas diving
into the blue currents.
I walked in Istanbul
before the bombs,
strolling along the
sharp edge of continents.

I wandered in Delhi
where the air was choked
by the smoke of humanity,
in Mumbai where the
holy waters were fouled
and the tormented poor were
stacked upon one another.

I stood on the parched
plains in South Africa
with the elephants
before they were felled,
beside the rhinoceros
before it was felled.

I have marveled in the naves
of a thousand empty cathedrals,
and ran my hands over
the carved marble of
the dissolving Taj Mahal.

I have seen the jungles of Panama
along the shores of Lake Gatun
I recall bays that were filled
with swirling schools of fish,
and trees where birds sang,
before the only sound
we could hear was the
labored breathing of the planet.

Awake on This Early Winter Morning

for Elizabeth Janeway

The nineteenth of
December, and our
bit of hillside bears
a new white shawl.

This morning it was
still darkness at seven,
the temperature no more
than eight degrees.

It is a cold that makes
a skeleton of a man,
when the north wind
sends needles thru the air.

The Warner River
is running like it is
early spring, straining
its banks with the rush
of last week's rains.

Brushstrokes of foam
add texture to form.
Big rocks along the bank
are wearing their new
crystal skirts, and in

The low and slow places
clean sheets of ice are
silently struggling
against the current to
set the table of winter.

Arrhythmias

for the good people at Concord Hospital- 5 Aug 2020

It would be easy
to hate this place,
How very tiny we feel
within the enormity of it.

But it has taken us
into its rooms.
Set us apart
where we can watch,
The nurses and technicians
of all names, festooned
in their pinks and yellows,
their cheerful cartoon prints.

They have determined to
care for the afflicted and
the stricken among us.

They make the measures
and the counts, stay awake
the long nights, while we
attempt rest between
the lifeless walls,
nodding off
to the songs of crickets
in their machines,

As we pause on the
landings of our long descent.
And bargain with the
dealer of our decrepitude.
It would be easy
to hate this place.
The fluorescent evenings
and disheveled sleep.

The bins of things
wrapped in plastic.
Our clothes folded
into an uneasy slumber,
inside a borrowed drawer.

You see, we do not
want to come here,
but we must. Driven
by that familiar fear,
The one which makes us
who we have always been.

We do not wish to
grow frail and feeble,
In need of the others,
who will mark our path.

So we resent it all,
the tubing and linens.
The taking of deep breaths.
The lying still
attempting to heal.

It would be easy
to hate this place,
Thinking of the bed
at home half empty, as

We take notice of what
minutes appear like
in passing.

At Davisville, New Hampshire

Here is the place I have found,
of fertile earth between tumbled stone.

Where old men lean thick arms
upon the tails of pick-ups,
on Autumn mornings and others,
and settle the matters of a day.

Where water spills from mountains,
over and down between hills.
and breaths, on winter nights
are seized by the gelid air.

Where the firmament
and all of its tiny lights,
lie upon the reach of treetops.

Where we can be with our aloneness,
at rest with its bottomless still,
and inhabit the life which inhabits us.

Dancers

Even as we live, it is
the dead we romance.
Leading them onto
the ballroom floor.

Placing a soft hand on
the swale of their backs.
We guide them in
slow and careful circles.
Over the lacquered wood.
Our cheeks pressed to theirs.

There is something
about that cold.
And the eyes.
Like unlit rooms.

We mourn them.
We sing them all the
sad and luscious songs.

They mourn us as well.
Watching from a balcony,
in the hall of our believing.
It is something
they will confess to us
someday.
Just after
asking us to dance.

Human History

In memory of Howard Zinn

It's a sad life
in a sad world

Where few
know the truth

And no one
will say it.

Squandering the precious
Defying death

We destroy
all we touch

Singing our songs
as we go.

Intelligent Design

for Christopher Hitchens

I cannot give
much credence
to divine
intervention,

Even at the
risk of my
defying
a redemption.

But I have faith
that it would
be wholly
mistakable,

To endorse any
god who'd make
a bone that
was breakable.

Life Now

It is not so different, really.
There are oaks and wildflowers,
and stones in our garden.
In the house where we sleep,
there is a case of books,
and they are our books.
The sunlight is most
beautiful in the early morning
just before the world gets busy.
There is work to be done
during each of our days, as well.
Work which makes us feel
tired and contented.

There is also water.
Not empty and still,
but thin and silken over
and amidst the big rocks.
All the long day and night
it makes a sound like wind.
It travels while our travels
have ended, Here.
There is a stately heron, who
comes to fish in the noon.
Yesterday I saw the hummingbird,
only minutes after I had reached
to hang his red feeder.

I was pleased at his arrival.
I spent a small time wondering,
how he knew where to find us,
just as he had done in
all those green summers,
far away.

Some of My Friends

Some of my friends
are becoming concerned.
About lumps where there
were none before.
Some thing which
does not look right.
Their comforts
undermined by
pains sharp or dull.
The need to draw breath
into deeper places.

Some are feeling vulnerable.
Their eyes are clouding.
words appearing to dissolve.
Sounds soft and muffled.
Some of my friends
need procedures and
further testing.
They will have to
travel to someplace
far and unfamiliar
and wait.

They will try to recall
when sleep came easy.

Now they might have
to be kept overnight,

have blood let by
girls named Betty.
Lie beneath beams
which will turn their
skin to rice paper.
All of their functions
will be distilled
to graphs and digits.

Some of my friends
seem to be wearing out.
Their pink becoming gray.
Their tightness loosened.
Some will be told today.

The Blue Heron

Within the depiction
which is this river,

The Blue Heron is composed.

In the moving world,
like the rock which
is his perch,

He must be the stillness.

He knows that what
he needs, will come.

He must be ready for it.

This morning's rain runs
off the slate of his back.

He understands, somehow.

The rain is the river, and
The river is the fish, and

The fish is himself.

The Book of Prophecy

I have been given
a datebook I cannot use.
It's a handsome thing.
Unpretentious, portable
and prepared for utility.
I even like its deep red cover,
which encases a future
I hope to see.

There is a blue ribbon I
could use to separate the
what has been, from the
what might be.

If I cannot find
someone in need of it, it
will have to remain barren.
Forever trapped by
a measure of time
it cannot escape.

The fortunate truth is that
I have a nice black one.
Soft and supple, perfect
for a back pocket or a
small corner of my nightstand,
and already populated by
my anticipations.

In a year's time, it will be
worthless and worn, papers
curled and consumed by
The totality of one man's
blue scribblings, and his hope
of making the future unforgettable.

The Man from an Unknown Place

Along the waterfront
in Old Bombay,
Beside the
Gateway of India,
Stood a man, dressed
in a black kurta pajama,
who asked where
I was from.
I said Boston, and
He said he
had never heard
of it.
I said, How
about New York?
He just said,
"No."

The Master Makes a Line

for Henri Matisse

My youth made
dancers move.
The curtain up,
beauty and poise
spinning within
the purple shades
of candles.
With my oils
I made them delicate
and strong, possessed of
inexhaustible youth.
Then there were
the ladies,
hundreds of them,
each one anxious
to recline before me.
Now I sit,
captured in this room,
betrayed by clocks.
Legs all but useless,
hands twisted as knots.
I must ask
my young girl
to strap a stick
to my arm, and
coax open the
bottle of ink.

I will show her
how it can be,
that a man can still
possess his gift.
That even a single line,
can become
a miracle.

To the Generals

for Gregory Riordan Moran

You must take.
It is your nature.

You must
take down
take away
take leave.

You must
empty and spend,
even waste.

We have come to see
You will not be denied.
But please is all I can say.

Do Not Take My Son.

Not his legs or arms,
Not an eye or thumb,
Not his heart or his mind.

He is not yours to spend.

Should you insist,
you should know,

I could not face
one day more, knowing
that I had let you do it.

Together and Waiting

The people in the waiting room at the hospital
cannot help but wonder just what is wrong
with everyone else.

The old woman in the borrowed wheelchair.
The man with the bandaged right hand.
The brown child whose mother is crying.

Someone has taped paper flowers to the wall.

A person in a green outfit will come for them soon.
They will learn, one at a time, the names of

The old woman in the borrowed wheelchair.
The man with the bandaged right hand.
The brown child whose mother is crying.

They all just want to be O.K.,
for the person in the green outfit to tell them so.
Then they can be happy again, happy
to be gone from the waiting room at the hospital.

And they can forget
the colors of the paper flowers taped to the wall
and the names they had learned one at a time.

Boating Through Jabalpur's Marble Canyons

We were eight
in a blue rusty boat,
Rowed slowly through
the up river canyons
of the Marble Falls, pulled
by three pair of slight men,
and another who pointed put
the details in the stone cascades.

High on a ledge, a small boy
and a smaller one as well,
yelled to us words that became
lost among their echoes.
The guide said the elder boy
would jump into the river
for 20 rupees (a nickel).
Thoughtfully, the offer
was considered, then
I said, tell them both
to jump.

What Color is Blue?

There are
those strands
of our reality
which defy our
words.

Limply, they
render answers,
Which simply
refuse
to appease.

I thought that
I knew blue,
Until I chanced
to sail on the
Mediterranean.
Now the bluest
of skies only
disappoints.
It makes me blue
to think about it.

Trapped in
the cage
of our senses,
All is but
air and light,

In a sea of
things which
move inside us,
in colors we are
unfit to describe.

For My Farmer's Daughter

for Karen

She says she
hates the gardening,
but she loves the
new greens and all
their tender blossoms.
It is something like
how she hates the
winter, but loves the
magic that is snow, falling
and falling all afternoon.

In the autumn she
loves how the hills
slowly surrender to
the rising color,
but she is
disquieted by all the
death, and the utterances
of loss expressed by the
drying crackle of litter.

Maybe it is
the steep recall in a
pain felt in the knees,
or how the soil
finds its way into
the swirl of a fingertip.

Maybe it's the short
light, and deepening cold,
maybe time spent to
fret over whether the
birds of our summer
are safe somewhere, and
Wondering through
many November days,
who is feeding nectar to
our ruby-throated children
on their long, long descent
down the hemisphere.

I remind her that
she is a farmer's daughter.
I remind her how once
she spent the long flat days
defying the Minnesota wind,
tending to pens filled with
eggs and white chickens.

And she explains
that it was her imagination
that came along to save her,
one purple day when she
was very young, and first
noticed that the sky was
a giant over her head, and
the roads in every direction
seemed to go the very
same place.

So, now we
are of that age when
complaint is a currency,
where nothing at all
seems the way we think
we remember it.

But, we have found
a place and it is ours,
where we must be grateful
for even January, and for
the line of black beneath
our nails, and the ache
in our knees which reminds
us we are alive, and that
the gardens we've made
beckon to be watered,
yet again.

On the Occasion of the Funeral of Donald Hall

at South Danbury, New Hampshire 30 June 2018

Praise be to the men
who find their place
and are content there,
Who understand the
treasures of silence
and small things,

Who can sing with echoes
and make their harmonies
along the wrinkles of time.
And praise be to the men
who press flowers into books
for strangers to find
long after they are gone.

Some Instructions

When my time comes.
Don't lay me in a box
with long bronze handles.
Don't comb my hair
the way you always
thought it should go
and lay my head on satin.
Don't polish my shoes.
Don't surround me
with grand bouquets.
Flowers die too soon.
Don't embrace one another
or blot the grief
from your eyes.
I will not have it.
There should be
no coffee, no cakes.
No one sing Amazing Grace.
And please, no churches,
no suggestions of the
mysterious will of
a god I deny.
I am not going home and
I will not rest in peace.
There can be no
peace in extinction.
Be certain that
I did not go willingly. Yet,
forego your misgivings.

Act as you will, as you must.
I will not raise up
a single objection, only
Be sure to have someone say
That given the chance,
I would have stayed a bit longer.